LOUDER THAN HEARTS

Louder Than Hearts

Zeina Hashem Beck

❧

BAUHAN PUBLISHING

PETERBOROUGH NEW HAMPSHIRE

2017

Library of Congress Cataloging-in-Publication Data
Names: Hashem Beck, Zeina, author.
Title: Louder than hearts : poems / Zeina Hashem Beck.
Description: Peterborough, New Hampshire : Bauhan Publishing, 2017.Identifiers: LCCN 2016058355 (print) | LCCN 2017001134 (ebook) | ISBN 9780872332348 (softcover : acid-free paper) | ISBN 9780872332355 (ebook)Classification: LCC PR9570.L43 H375 2017 (print) | LCC PR9570.L43 H375 2017 (ebook) | DDC 823/.92--dc23
LC record available at https://lccn.loc.gov/2016058355

You can contact Zeina on zeinabeck@gmail.com.
http://www.zeinahashembeck.com/
Follow her on Facebook and Twitter (@zeinabeck)

Book design by Kirsty Anderson
Cover Design by Henry James

BAUHAN
PUBLISHING LLC
PO BOX 117 PETERBOROUGH NEW HAMPSHIRE 03458
603-567-4430
WWW.BAUHANPUBLISHING.COM
Follow us on Facebook and Twitter – @bauhanpub

MANUFACTURED IN THE UNITED STATES OF AMERICA

For my Marwan, Leina, & Aya
For my parents & my aunts
For Rana

To our broken languages
& our broken cities

CONTENTS

A Note on Arabic Words and Transliteration

Louder than Hearts contains Arabic words and expressions, most of which are explained in a glossary at the end of this book.

Depending on the feel/tone of each poem, Arabic words have been transliterated using different systems. For most, a "traditional" transliteration system has been used (example: Qur'an, *lahm bi 'ajeen*). Other words have been written using Arabizi (example: *3amto* instead of *'amto*). Arabizi comes from the combination of the words "Arabic" and "Englizi" (English); it uses numbers to represent sounds that are specifically Arabic, and has become well-known online and in texting.

Where the words are very familiar in a certain form, I've kept that form (example: Eid rather 'Eid or 3eid).

BROKEN GHAZAL: SPEAK ARABIC

I write in English the way I roam foreign cities—full of street light
& betrayal, until I find a coffee shop that speaks Arabic.

If we were born in the cities we long for, Love—Paris, Prague, New York—
what languages would they have taught us to speak? Arabic

says the best singers are the peddlers. & the Qur'an,
would it still lift us if it didn't speak Arabic?

Sure, there is always Lennon, but I wonder if we would have found
Sheikh Imam, who reminds us the wound is awake & love speaks Arabic,

who reminds us no one can colonize a river, & the tyrant
is always afraid of the poet, especially if she speaks Arabic.

They say people who grow up in two languages have stronger
memories, & they can hear the birds on the balconies speak Arabic,

& they know a mountain of orange life jackets looks like
spring, though it won't revive the dead, who speak Arabic

but no longer need a visa, or translation. & you, Zeina, what else
can you do but whisper to these broken lines, *Speak. Speak Arabic.*

1
SHAFAQ
شفق

I DREAMT WE THREW BREAD CRUMBS

I dreamt we threw bread crumbs
in the sea, waited to catch
a glimpse of our hunger, our hope,
rising out of this dark.

You fished out a tin can;
before we ate it
you told me to listen to the prayer
inside it—our prayer.

You mapped my body in chalk
on the sidewalk. My longing
was ruby-colored. I wore it
around my neck, and everything
was drunkenness and dance, every day
a kind of drowning—

the *shawarma* on the skewers,
the plastic roses in the children's hands,
the antennas scribbled across the sky.
Only the clotheslines knew
of our leaving, our returning,
and they wept.

AFTER THE EXPLOSIONS
For Tripoli, Lebanon, August 2013

After the explosions, I've been having ash-dreams;
everything's grey, even the children's pencil cases.
September with its play of light and possibilities
burst in unnoticed. My dead cousin
comes to me smiling, tries to pinch me, laughs.
Two days after the explosions, the pharmacy parrot
who wouldn't keep quiet was found alive;
he doesn't speak, but meows from time to time.
The owner jokes, "This country will have him
barking soon." The trees seem to remember
the human parts in their branches.
Some elevators have sprung out of their places
like frightened hearts. I try not to think
about the three children who died holding
each other in a van, after a day at the beach.

I take my mind past the broken balconies,
into my friend's shattered house, stare at the frame
still hanging on the cracked wall: a fishing boat, a calm
sea. The volunteers are sweeping the street, the kid
who sells chewing gum is helping. The survivor
with an eye patch says it sounded like glass rain.
My aunt sings good-bye to her son from the window,
the red *tarboosh* on his coffin in the distance,
her white handkerchief taking flight.

LISTEN

You're telling yourself he's fine. *He didn't go to the mosque today.*
Again, your mother screams. Your father is running up,
is down, the whole town is down. You call,
praying. You call (the goddamn line),
try to forget your brother might be—
God. You run to the balcony;
You heard that? Is it?
You shake. Again
a boom;
That—
hear?
Did you?
It explodes,
the mosque, this Friday,
the laundry, the domes of
boys' arms, the sumac. Noon
flows, ebbs. The Chiclets in the street.
Viscous, this August heat, the city, the day.
The sea, still. The children, the figs almost bursting.
Not even gods could, who could have possibly—I mean listen.

Not even gods could, who could have possibly—I mean listen:
the sea, still; the children; the figs almost bursting,
viscous—this August heat; the city, the day
flows, ebbs; the Chiclets in the street
boys' arms, the sumac, noon,
the laundry, the domes of
the mosque, this Friday
it explodes
did you
hear
that?
A *boom,*
you shake again,
You heard that? Is it?
God. You run to the balcony,
try to forget your brother might be
praying, you call, the goddamn line
is down, the whole town is down, you call
again, your mother screams, your father is running up,
you're telling yourself he's fine. He didn't go to the mosque today.

YOU FIXED IT

And if the compass broke you fixed it, fastened
the pencil to it with a rubber band,
and if there was no hot water you fixed it, learnt
to sit on that plastic stool in the bathroom
and count, and if it was too cold outside
you fixed it, and there was the smell of burnt
lemon on the brazier, or the *click*
click click of the gas heater.
And if you were bored you fixed it, learnt to cut
paper and color the scraps, learnt to write
on the walls, and if you wrote on the walls you
fixed it, scrubbed them with your mom who yelled
at your big brother who what on earth
was he doing just watching? And if the TV blurred
you fixed it, adjusted the antenna to catch
those Japanese cartoons translated into Arabic
on the Syrian channel, and if the cartoons
hadn't begun you fixed it, danced
to those nationalistic Syrian songs about Hafiz, repeated
ya hala ya hala ya hala heh. And if you didn't have enough
books you fixed it, read that French-Arabic dictionary the size
of your torso, stared at the words *crépuscule* and شفق.
And if you tripped on the missing tile you fixed it,
learnt to count your steps in the dark
afternoon without electricity, and if there was no
electricity you fixed it, gauged
how dark it was by whether or not you could see

your thumb, and if you couldn't see your thumb
you fixed it, got the candle from under the sink,
and if the sink was leaking you fixed it, tied
a cloth to the pipe, and if the pipe burst
you fixed it, pressed your palms
against the hole in the wall until
Mom called the grocer to call the butcher to call
the plumber next to him, and if there was a hole
in your sock you fixed it, learnt to fold it
under your big toe. And if your window shattered
you fixed it, taped cardboard to the frame,
and if someone died you fixed it by telling stories
about how crusty their *lahm bi 'ajeen* was,
and if the *lahm bi 'ajeen* was too crusty
you fixed it by dipping it in the tahini,
and if your sorrow hardened you fixed it
by dipping it in seawater, and if your country
hardened, if your country hardened you fixed it
by dipping it in song.

MY TOWN
After Buddy Wakefield and Will Evans

My town got in a car and sped and shot my cousin
dead, drove back, shot again to make sure.
His last word was *ummi* and my town
is also my *ummi*.

My town is cheap. They call her
"the mother of the poor." Yehya the carpenter
can duplicate a Pottery Barn bedroom
for quarter the price. My town is the mother

of the poor, her children sell Chiclets
and *barazeq* on the streets, on the streets one boy
kept telling me, "I go to school," and I said,
"Never stop," and one day he did.
I wonder whether he has been taught to place
the blade of a pencil sharpener under
his tongue, spit it out in an offender's face.

My town is the mother of soap,
she crafts it out of olive oil,
adds honey or flower petals or herbs,
adds bullets when it's a boy, firecrackers
when children pass tests,
adds car honks when it's a *'arooss*.

My town likes to boast she is the mother
of the North, which in Lebanese also means "left,"
which, she likes to remind me, is where the heart is.

My town is the mother of stories. She says
a great snake lies in the darkness
of her ancient citadel, says she was once

the mother of orange orchards
(inhales to remember their scent),
that she is much more than her name, which means

"three cities." "Ha!" she laughs, "I have seen
the Assyrian the Persian the Roman the Byzantine the Caliphate
the Seljuk the Crusader the Mamluk the Ottoman and the French."
When I ask her what more she will see, she falls
silent, asks me what I'd like to eat.

My town tastes like *kaak* and falafel and *chocolat mou* and burnt books.
My town tastes like *Allahu Akbar* on a Eid morning, which never
tasted like fear, my town is the mother

of fear. It has been growing in her womb
for years, and she doesn't know who
it will look like when it's born, whether
it will speak in tongues unknown
to her. Perhaps she is hoping for a stillborn.

GHAZAL: THE DEAD

You had to visit them before the living, the dead.
In your new Eid shoes, at dawn—a time for reviving the dead.

Your father stared at his mother's tombstone, lifted
his palms like food, like forgiving the dead.

Your mother went a little later to her brother's grave,
said nothing hurt more that this—outliving, the dead.

You asked about the men chanting to Allah on the plastic chairs—
Were they real? Were they grieving the dead?

You wanted to linger, to listen, to dance beside
their voices, this believing, the dead.

Your mother pushed you into the red Renault shimmering
like a drop of blood in the sunlight, leaving the dead.

Some nights, the shadows wash up on your bedroom walls. You tell them
your name, ask them for stories—they have ways of giving, the dead.

MESSAGE FROM MY AUNT ON HER SON'S DEATH ANNIVERSARY

My aunt, the one who has lost a son
to a shooting on the street, the one slowly losing
her sight, sends me voice messages and emoticons,
prayers like *A fortress, my love,*
protect you from harm in all directions—
above and below you, behind and before you.

Today, the emoticon is an orange.
Perhaps it's a mistake. Perhaps she means
a kiss, or a heart, or a flower,
her eyes and aging fingers failing her.

But perhaps she means the fruit, remembers
how she used to sing me that song
where I was the orange she wanted
to peel and eat and not share with anyone,

remembers how much I love sour winter oranges,
the way they are round and whole, yet break
into the many bright crescents hidden beneath their skin.

Perhaps she's saying what she always says
when she opens her arms and walks toward me,
I was telling myself you must have arrived.
The whole town smells of oranges when you are here.

PIZZA WITH LIGHTBULB

Mama made the best Arabic pizza: soft, thick,
with olives, mushrooms, *ash'awan* cheese,
ketchup instead of pizza sauce.
But that night there was something
different about it. We knew
one should never complain
about homemade food,
so we crunched and swallowed,
washed it down with Pepsi,
until she heard the glass shards
under our teeth. She opened the oven,
found out the light in there had
burst. The doctor on the phone
said the only side effect
would be our asses lighting up
at night. It was a practical thing, after all,
to turn into lightning bugs
with the electricity gone
from midnight until 6 a.m.

3AMTO

1 Najwa (or Consolation)

God will cure this cancer in my chest. I will go alone
to hajj this year and tell Him. He listens. Yes,
alone. No one will dare ask an old dying woman
about her male guardian. Here's the key
to the drawer next to my bed. My sapphire ring
is in there. You can also have my mink coat.
Stop crying. If only I could
take Coco with me—that poor parrot
has been plucking out her feathers.
Open her cage door, *habibti.* She likes to walk
around the living room in the afternoons.
Slit the window. I can tell you don't like
this smell of bird food and tobacco. Stop crying,
switch on the fan. I remember when you were little,
you cried every time your mom left you here, hid
under this small table, or in the big white jar in the salon.
Living is such a strange thing. I've buried
two children, you know. Do you think they'll let me
bring my *shisha* to Mecca? Stop crying, *habibti.*
Turn on the TV and let's watch that show
with all those big men beating each other up.

2 Labibah (or Reason)

My eyelashes are falling into the *fattoush* these days.
My children call them blessings, *barakat*. Forgive me
if you find a few in your plate. I can't complain,
hamdillah, the operation went well. The doctors told me
the gallbladder is shaped like a pear—made me think
they were plucking it out. The gallstones are bright,
almost beautiful, almost good for a necklace.
Come visit me more often, not just
when I'm sick. You used to tell me you couldn't wait
to drive a car, so you could come over every day. Remember?
I used to answer, "By then you wouldn't want to."
I'm old and I understand. You're here now, and I know
how to sew your visits together seamlessly. *Hamdillah.*
My eyes love to see you. Drive here more often.
I will make *wara2 3enab*, let you eat it from the pot.

3 Ismat (or Virtue)

Every woman should learn how to cut her hair short
and curse like a man. Ask your cousins
about that time they were late, how I flung
the shutters open, threw all kinds
of insults at them, as they looked up from the street.
When they were younger, I sometimes tied them with rope
to the kitchen chairs. How else was I supposed to get things done
around the house? I stopped dyeing my hair and wearing perfume
a long time ago. Once, I had big curls and pink pants and a waist so tiny
it could fit into a ring. Fuck that. Here I am in an old photo:

the baby I'm holding is you. I left to Australia
before you turned one. I cried so much
as I bent over your cot, kissed you in your sleep.
You had the smallest baby earrings, the most beautiful
baby ears, *yil3an abooki*. I believe you understood
what I whispered to you that evening.

4 Sakina (or Calm)

Allo?   Hi *ya 3uyuni inti*   you are
my eyes my eyes my eyes
I miss you   so much   kiss your dad
for me   what was that you said?   sorry
the line isn't good   yes it's very late
here   but never too late to hear your voice
that's fine no don't   hang up   night and day
are the same   to me   youth and old age
sea and mountain   all will be   flattened
made equal   in front of   Allah   yes my hand
is swollen yes   it hurts but   I've learnt to stay   still
and breathe inside   all this pain life is one deep
sigh   my love *akh*   remember
we don't live   a minute more not a minute   more
than what was written for us   everything
is written   now tell me   about your children.

5 Yathrib (or Light)

Everything changes, *ya 3amto*, everything. See
how the bones at my knuckles bulge, hurt. I can't
make proper *kibbeh* anymore, can't tame
the meat and bulgur into shape like I used to.
My neighbors talked about my *kibbeh*—its scent
from the grill on the balcony, its heart
full of fat. Remember to eat it with your hands,
dip it in *laban*. Never with knife and fork
like those people who call themselves civil.

I miss walking on the beach. Your mother and I
once paced the pier in August. I sweat under
my hijab, looked at the sea: like oil, it shone,
was still. I was eating it with my eyes.
I told your mom I wished I could just
jump in there, so she pushed me into the water,
made it look like an accident. I swam back
to the shore, pretended to be ashamed
at how I'd slipped. I thanked her later
as I dried off and sipped 7UP and—
what's it called? That red cool thing?
Grenadine.

My name, Yathrib, sounds strange,
ancient to you, but it means "City of Lights;"
it's where the Prophet (Peace Be Upon Him)
is buried. Don't worry about me. Bullets or no bullets,
I won't leave my house. I've got pillows, you know—
one for my back, one for my neck,
one underneath my knee. Do you still
recite the Qur'an I've taught you?
Repeat the verses every night
before you sleep. The one that shields the most
is *Ayat al-Kursi*. Don't forget.

DISMANTLING GRIEF

is never a straightforward thing. Start
with a handful of earth, scattered over the wrapped
body lowered into the ground. Move

back to when you were tying your shoelaces
before the phone rang—the *Allo?*, the silence.
"Are we all martyrs?" writes Darwish.

Months after the burial, he will come back
to ask about the bullets, the holes in his chest. Tell him,
"You were eating falafel on the street." Try

to stay still until almost nothing is left
but the sound of water inside the building walls.
The beauty of sunsets will hurt. Fade

the red. Like a matchstick,
you will break, burn. Go back
to that afternoon when you were both ten,

learning how to make a circle. Remember
how he taught you to steady your hand. Go out
on the balcony. Sip your morning coffee in the cold, look—

the paper on the parked car says "For Sale"
and Julia is singing, "I pray for you." This is a good day
to run. Your shoes are in the closet. Get them.

2
YA'ABURNEE
يقبرني

RELENTLESS

"Stop writing about war," he said. "Stop
writing about borders and blood. Stop writing
about revolutions and revolvers, about cities,
rooftops with antennas and snipers.
Stop writing about bread
and barefoot children with their dark
skin, their hair blond from too much sun.
Stop telling the story of how your friend
bought hats for them and gave them out
from her car window, saying *put this on*
put this on. Stop telling the story of the gates
your grandfather painted on his wall
to remember, and the gates he painted
on his heart to forget. For God's sake stop
writing about religion, I'm tired
of minarets and crosses, even the prayers
are tired and want to sleep. Just write
some shade for me to sit in."

So I drew him a tree without roots,
a street with enormous wings, and said, "Here
is a tree that cannot be uprooted,
a street that will take flight
before it explodes." And I drew myself
some mud, two strong legs, a clothesline
upon which to hang my drenched words,
see what this sunlight would make of them,
and black birds on a fence
like the pattern of a *kaffiyeh*.

THIRTY-TWO AND IN A DIFFERENT COUNTRY

In the afternoon, the soldiers swarm
the building walls, like spiders. Every night

you are ten, you stand behind the glass door
of the balcony, until you begin to see them,

shadowlike, about to jump
over the railing. This is when you start to run,

and it's always into your parents' old house,
and you're always in your pajamas, barefoot.

You try to hide under the bed first, then realize
it's too obvious. You try the closet, slip

behind your mother's dresses.
They're in the living room now, and you

can see them, as if your mind were a camera—
the rifles, the helmets, the dark green

uniforms. You sneak into the kitchen,
open the cupboards under the sink,

you wish you could turn into air, into salt.
You hear the boots, the flower vase

flung onto the floor. You make a final sprint
to the bathroom. Laughter. Someone spits.

You decide, *Bathtub*. The voices get closer.
You look at the small window, think, *Jump*.

You tell yourself you are thirty-two,
you are thirty-two and in a different country.

YA'ABURNEE

when my daughter, proud,
carries her milk tooth
in a plastic bag
the graffiti in my head reads

IN THIS BAG, MY SON

when she asks
how many suns
so the world could shine

MORE THAN 500
DEAD

when she asks how many
skies

THOUSANDS
OF HOUSES

when she brings me
flowers she has picked
their heads floating
in a bowl

RUN!
(sprayed in vibrant colors)

when she points
to an image of Mary
says *This is the Mona Lisa*

MOSUL

when she swings
from an olive tree

LAND

when she says she likes
her grandmother's soup best
in red

HUNGER

when she tells me *ya'aburnee*
because she thinks it's the best love
term one could ever use
(I say it to her all the time)
my mind turns

BLANK

I shout
No, never,
        GOD
forbid

when she asks what *ya'aburnee*
means, asks again, insists
I explain

YA'ABURNEE

means parents
grow old and die before
their children do

when she says,

IT'S THE SADDEST DAY

when you don't sleep next to me

I know she means

STAY

means

LOSS

means

HOME

TAHTARIQ/BURNING

Barra—out

> we chanted
> outside the American embassy

Hurra—free

> we marched
> to protest the bombing
> of Iraq

Matar—rain

> there was no rain, but the tear gas fell.
> A woman ran into the street with onions,
> gave them out to the students. "Inhale," she told me,
> grabbed my arm. "Here, into the alley. This,

Bayti—my house

Allah—God

> be with you."
> Someone carried a photo of Che,
> someone said we must stop this

Ihtilal—occupy

    the embassy. My father called

Allo allo

    I didn't answer.
    In the evening we lit candles
    on the street, sang

Kulluna—all of us

    sometimes you are not sure why
    you laugh at funerals.
    The next day the newspapers
    showed a picture of a student

Tanzof—bleeding

    from the head, her arms open.
    In a university hall another
    student ran and screamed
    Baghdad! Baghdad

Tahtariq—burning.

AND STILL, THE SUN
After Pablo Neruda's "Walking Around"

I happen to be tired of being

> an Arab. My worst, my best childhood memory is listening
> to the news every morning, in my dad's car. I waited
> for the tunnel—the interrupted signal, the mountain silence.

The smell of barbershops makes me wail.

> I skip the headlines about the CIA tortures, the elections, the war—
> the newspaper words crawl up my arms like black ants. I read about
> Mercury, how it might help me speak, how Venus might orbit love my way.

I happen to be tired of my feet and my nails

> and *zaatar*, and olive oil, and the scent of bread from the bakery downstairs.
> The siren outside weeps into my window, the distance. The coffee
> rises in the kettle, the cigarette smoke burns my eye.

Nevertheless it would be delightful

> to believe all those things my *teita* said about *Amerka*—
> everyone there is civilized, and free. And they have street
> numbers, and they know how to queue up when they're supposed to.

I don't want to go on being a root in the dark.

A black friend once told me, "Black is like
Third World, you know, like Arab."
(how we carry names and meanings)

I don't want for myself so many misfortunes—

the way Mezzeh will always mean Syrian prison,
will invoke that TV image of a man with blue swollen legs.
My mother said he was among the lucky ones. I was ten.

This is why Monday burns like petroleum—

for what else burns here?
Houses, and childhood, and olive trees. And still,
the sun, and all this laughter and singing.

And it pushes me into certain corners, into certain moist houses—

My friend who grew up in Syria says Mezzeh
has beautiful cactus trees, says she first kissed there,
first smoked, talks her way into the heart of Damascus.

There are brimstone-colored birds and horrible intestines

>and cyclamens on the mountains of my childhood—
>pink and fragrant like newborn babies
>among the rocks. Here, open mouths. Here, leaf hearts.

I walk around with calm, with eyes, with shoes,

>although the sound of a washing machine
>in the middle of the night made me scream, shake, ask
>if we had a gun in the house, if we knew how to use it.

TERROR/MATHEMATICS
After the beheading of 21 Christian Egyptians in Libya, February 2015

Try calculated, think math.
Capture & + the numbers,
– the Muslims. 21 is what you are

left with, which is 3×7. Any multiple of 3
is blasphemous, is $\sqrt{\text{all}}$ evil,
& we will / its neck open.

Islam is an X
in an equation we never
want you to solve. A % of you

will stop eating breakfast. Sure, there is the grief
of the mothers, who will pull at their hair,
+ the fathers, who will cover their faces with dirt,

& this can't be ÷, like ∞,
but who has time for pain ≫ the sea,
which we will turn red. The killer/killed

ratio is 1:1, + the orator, who names the horror.
Color too is used in this ∑. Kneel now, facedown,
& we will show you Death$^{\text{Orange.}}$

You can keep your // universe of Love. We $\vec{x}$
ourselves to Paradise, which is $\perp$ and exact.
It's simple. Try this:

$$[(\text{Allah} + \text{Blood}) \times (\text{Scream} + \text{Akbar})] = Y^{\text{Fear}}$$
& this $\Rightarrow \not\exists$ a God here,
but surely, $\exists$ a Hell.

INSIDE OUT
For Gaza, July 2014

people inside out
on the streets in their loved ones'
arms people screaming
in football stadiums
my friend's mom in Gaza is cheering
for Brazil & Holland
all that orange
burning almost
a sunrise all that
smoke
there's an old woman
who dies holding
her spoon waiting
for *Iftar*
which comes but so do
the rockets
& the news
Brazil loses to Germany 7–1
ABC News confuses
Israel & Palestine
the whole dichotomy
occupied/
occupier inside
out
out
Holland loses

a girl not yet
one
wrapped in a flag
flags wrapt
around cars necks shoulders heads
in Gaza God
is the eyes
of a little doll kicked
among the rubble
eyes follow a ball
kicked in midair
a roof collapses
houses inside out
one bride postpones
her wedding
the game goes into
extra time
shelters there are no shelters
shield yourself with
your hands your voice
i haven't slept since
yesterday writes Anas *go ahead*
& bombard july 13th
he dies the next day
a player kisses a trophy
his wife his son
a mother
kisses a dead child

grief inside out
is resistance
the crowds wave
at the victorious team
a whole family stands
on the roof waving
at the enemy's planes

GHAZAL: THIS *HIJRA*
For Mosul and Sinjar, 2014

The little girls have eyes that will forever weave this *hijra*.
On mountains and in villages people eat their homes and leave—this, *hijra*.

My father once told me about a spider that spun a web across a cave
where the Prophet hid. He said, "The spider saved him. Believe this *hijra*."

Take the blankets and put the children in the trunk of the Toyota.
Tell them about the kites they will fly to cleave this *hijra*.

I have been sold twenty-two times. Every time I desert my body
I remind myself the Tigris and the Euphrates will meet to grieve this *hijra*.

In this heat, we imagine angels with airplane wings, and water.
We call, "*Ya* Sayyab! Sing us the song of the rain, of this eve, this *hijra*."

The old man has stayed in his house. He walks from room to room, names
kettle, chair, mattress. He knows they're coming, but he can't conceive this: *hijra*.

The spider's spun a pattern that resembles a fire escape. "Run," it says, "zigzag
your way through. No web big enough here, no cave to deceive. This—*hijra*."

Baba insisted on my Arabic name. People suggested, "More modern, more
Western." But he said, "This, too, is parting (I'm Mustafa, not Steve). This, *hijra*."

GHAZAL: BACK HOME
For Syria, September 2015

Tonight a little boy couldn't walk on water or row back home.
The sea turned its old face away. Again, there was a *no, no,* back home.

Bahr is how we were taught to measure poetry,
bahr is how we've stopped trying to measure sorrow, back home.

"All that blue is the sea, and it gives life, gives life," says God to the boy
standing wet at heaven's gate—does he want to return, to go back home?

My friend who hates cooking has made that eggplant dish,
says nothing was better than yogurt and garlic and tomato, back home.

On the train tracks, a man shouts, "Hold me, hold me," to his wife,
bites her sleeve, as if he were trying to tow back home.

Thirteen-year-old Kinan with the big eyes says, "We don't want to stay in Europe."
"Just stop the war," he repeats, as if praying, *Grow, grow back, home.*

Habibi, I never thought our children would write HELP US on cardboard.
Let's try to remember how we met years ago, back home.

On our honeymoon we kissed by the sea, watched it
rock the lights, the fishing boats to and fro, back home.

NAMING THINGS
For refugees, September 2015

Angels—
we saw them on the railway, the street,
covered with dust.
We licked our fingers & wrote
رحلنا
on their wings.

Wings—
my daughter left them on her bed,
cried when she remembered.
We found a dead seagull by the sea,
before we took the inflatable boat,
so I plucked a feather for her.
She smiles, but still asks
about our cat.

Cats—
all your life you've loved them & yet
believed they brought you bad luck. Every time
we adopt one, we lose a vase, a soul, & now
a country. Let's sleep in that little alley
where the cats walk
on the edge of
~~refuge~~ refuse bins.

Country—
the trees will seem barren

will seem heavy with fruit
will make you cry, like onions.
Your eyes will be fine. Remember
the name your parents gave you
has plenty of shade. Rest in it.

Onions—
my kind of moon, the kind
you could cut through,
the kind you could eat. Not
that rubber globe in the sky,
its heart full of air.

The heart—
never learns
keeps coming back
to the same songs,
the same wars.

War—
hums, *I will make love
to you in a bed of blood & faith,*
will show you her lips,
hide her teeth, her money-scented
breath, the rust on her tongue, the children
underneath her fingernails.

Tongue—
they've burnt
Aeham's piano
on his birthday.
He has left Yarmouk for Germany.
Remember the vodka,
back when we were students,
drunk in your car? Our youth
is still in the backseat. The dust
was so beautiful; I watched it fall
all afternoon, in the sun.

The sun—
doesn't need us
is not a blanket
films us with its glare
do I look oh-so-cinematic
more dramatic in this light,
mr. le photographe?
Do my eyes my hands
tell a story?

Stories—
I try to tell my boys
we are backpacking through Europe.
My great-grandmother, who had lost her mind
to old age, used to talk about a monster
in the trees. Chops people off & cooks them.

Like this, she'd say, moving her fingers as if
she were rolling a sandwich, & I'd become
afraid. & hungry.

Hunger—
the sea is a cemetery.
That fish you grilled last night,
did it laugh? Did it say, *I have been feeding
on your children*? It tasted good
with olive oil & lemon & garlic.
My mother always said everything
(even the dead) tastes good
with olive oil & lemon & garlic.

Mother—
land
mother—
tongue
mama
told a journalist
she'd go back to the war
if they allowed me into Germany.
*No problem, just take her,
let her pass*, she said,
as she combed my hair.

My hair—
or is that seaweed? Grass?

Grass—
your father's clothes
will smell of him, as if he'd just
stepped out of them & went
to lie down underneath the grass.
Leave them there. They will grow
too heavy in the rain.

The rain—
fuck
even the rain, this
funeral song.
It, too, will go out to sea
& bury us.

Bury—
when I die,
you will recognize me by my tattoo.
I got it when I was twenty-three,
it says, و ما أطال النوم عمراً
"Sleep has never lengthened a life,"
& that is why we are those who love
watching the night, we call it سهر
& Leila comes over
every night for whiskey, laughs
& repeats *Ya Allah! Ya Allah!*

God—
is sometimes a camera,

sometimes has a nom de guerre,
but mostly he's that old drum
beating at the heart of my mother
language, giving me the urge to dance,
or a broken hip.

My hips—
are heavy
are child-bearing
child-killing
are lover
do not fit those
train windows
these fences
this escape this

Ra7eel—
so much in my *3arabi* depends
on *ra7eel* on

3awda—
akh ya baba
I have fallen in love
with Beckett, I stumble
on my Arabic inflections, confuse

subject & object,
but I have promised al-Mutanabbi
I will come back.

Promise—
some people are kind, say
Bienvenu, Welcome, أهلاً
here's some water, here's a toy,
a sandwich, here
away from slaughter & also
from my balconies, my bed, my books.
There is no space for me
to make love to you here.

Here—
Nina Simone sings
Got my liver, got my blood,
so here, despite the children sleeping
on the floor, & the tents, & the sea,
& much much more,
kiss me, for where else
do we carry home now, *habibi*,
if not on our lips?

3
AHWAK
أهواك

LOUDER THAN HEARTS AND *DERBAKKEHS*

The woman in me is thousands
of years old, her voice louder
than hearts and *derbakkehs*.

She calls her children from the farthest
room in the house, screams, *Yalla or else*,
says, *Eat your food and be grateful. Finish
your plate*. And despite all

the parenting books I've read,
the ones with instructions
like *Talk calmly to the child,
Stoop down to child eye level*,
she still comes out

yelling from her height
at my kids when they don't listen.
She gestures, brings thumb and index together,
threatens them with *Wallah wallah you'll see*,
never shows them. She screams

across corridors, from balconies, in playgrounds,
across land-mine fields, broken houses, wastelands.

Some days I manage to put her to sleep,
light her a cigarette, or pour her
a cup of coffee. Some days she boils
in my blood, says, *Out of my way*.
Some days I hold her in my arms,
rock her back and forth, let her cry.

THE WOMAN IN OUR HOUSE

I remember a portrait
in my parents' house—an Arab woman
in orange, her dress aflame,
her feet bare
on the leopard-print rug,
a filigree window to her left.
No one knew

who she was. My dad had bought her
because she looked like Mom—blue
eyes, white skin, short wavy hair.
Mom loved how her body
seemed sated; "all a-blossom,"
she'd say, "like the lilies to her right."

Dad bought lilies once, and Mom tossed
the flowers away, saying you can't
wrap a wound with petals.
Decades later, I found out

that woman was an Andalusian poet.
Her name, Wallada, meant
she would have many children. But she didn't.
She opened literary salons, embroidered
her lines on her sleeves, never
married. When I told Mom, asked her
where the portrait was, she cried,
said she'd thrown her away
a long time ago.

WALLADA BINT AL-MUSTAKFI SPEAKS

I walk the streets of Córdoba
with my hair, my poetry embroidered
on my sleeves, my lips a hunger
for you. Andalusian princess, I

open my palace to women who pine,
teach poetry even to my slaves, challenge men
to complete lines, defeat them.

And when I love you, I will come
to you under the cover of the night,
run through you like the Nile through Egypt.
And when you're unfaithful, I will recite
your treason to the town, shame
and banish you. And when you return,
I will forgive, tell my new lover-vizier
to allow you into the city again. I will marry

neither him nor you. I know my name
predicts I will bear many children, and I will,
but they will be born centuries after I die. Undefeated,
I will die on the same day the Berbers enter Córdoba.

MAJNUN
After Majnun Layla

Love is not complicated.
I die among the rocks, the beasts,
shaded by your memory, Layla.

Shaded by your memory,
I roam this desert, tear
at my clothes, ramble until
I hear someone call, *Layla.*

I hear someone call, *Layla,*
and words beat their wounded wings
out of my heart, my mouth. When travelers ask
what I write in the sand, I tell them I live
inside the letters of your name.

Only inside the letters of your name—L-a-y-l-a—
I wake. I am halved, like a line of poetry:
here the silence, the sun scorches, my grave
calls, offers no forgetting; here the night,
named after you, cloaks me with hope
to go near your tent again.

To go near your tent again, to kneel
facing you, not Mecca. My father took me
to the Prophet's grave once,
said, *Perhaps you'll find another song.*

I circled the *Kaaba*, prayed, *Layla, Layla.*
I don't want to heal from worshipping you—
let them call me *majnun.*

Call me *majnun*, Layla.
I freed gazelles from my trap
because they reminded me of you.
What food for those already dead
of hunger? Tell me, did he
kiss you in the morning?
Let me, then, dive into the dark
flame of this night, this *layla.*

ODE TO MY NON-ARABIC LOVER

I couldn't love you, you see, even though
I love you. Soon it will be too late, too dark,
even at midday, and I will forget
my English. It's one thing to make love
and say *yes* say *more*
in your language, but how will I ever translate
my Arab anger, my alliterations, those rough sounds
that scratch their way out of my throat,
which you will merely find sexy?
And yes I know you could learn
your Fairuzes and your Umm Kulthums,
your curse words, your Beiruts, your Niles,
your street names and your *yallas*. But what will happen when

I begin to lose this English I've trained myself to speak?
I'm already old and walk night corridors,
whispering things even I don't get
in a language you don't understand,
following sunlit Sundays to long tables
under the shade of grape vines and the smell
of raw meat and arak. You will get bored
of all these songs stamping their *dabkeh*
inside my head, *Walak ooff ooff ooff*
do not call me cruel,
say I love my language more than my love,
my love. I don't. You see?
I'm already tired and you already
mistranslate.

MY NON-ARABIC LOVER AND I TAKE THE TRAIN

We took a train to Prague tonight.
I kept saying *orloj* and *Kafka* and you
said *Oui, tout de suite, on arrive.*
I had never been on a train before, held on
to my ticket, looked out the window, couldn't
sleep. When the wheeled creature stopped,
we stepped down, found ourselves
in my hometown of Tripoli. I saw my father
crossing a street with his friend, ran
into his arms. He said he was going to buy new
shoes. I saw my mother, who told me
she had cut her hair short by herself, had nothing
to lose anyway, after what happened. I saw
my old school bus stop next to the café where
it used to drop me, saw Basma step out, still thirteen.
All the time I gasped, smiled, said hello, my heavy
northern accent sinking back into my tongue.
You followed, silent, watched the map of me unfold,
grow rivers and strange names and temples. *This way,*
I showed you, my arm like a small bridge, *this*
place, the best fatteh in town, explained
how it was made of chickpeas, bread, yogurt, tahini.
You asked me about the armed men in the street,
and I told you there was melted ghee on top of it,
there were roasted pine nuts. I could already taste it.

نوم

Tonight you said you couldn't sleep,
so I taught you how to trace

the word نوم. All the letters
in نوم sound gentle—nothing

guttural about it. Here, give me
your index. The first letter

is sharp, a right angle.
The second one curls

like a fetus. *Lie to me,*
lie to me. Hush now, focus.

The last letter, say it, *mm,*
will put you to sleep: see how

it starts to circle, goes left, then dips
like pain. Don't forget the point

above the first letter, a little beauty spot
like the ones strewn across my back, a black

pupil. Now shut your eyelids. I love
how long your dark eyelashes are.

KHANDAQ MON AMOUR

But what I really want
is to love you, kill you,
on this trench of a street—
a broken window, dark green shutters
overlooking that shell of a church,
the ghosts of thieves, of publishing houses,
of writers walking with their manuscripts in their arms.
No forgetting here, only making coffee and love
above the sounds of motorcycles and slogans for religions
that tear at each other with nails and heaven.
Think about that when your body longs for
my bare back, my long legs, my laughter. Here everything
has been stolen, killed, or survives.
There are no stairs in that building, and I
am watching from the last floor,
where the mosaics on the ground remain
untouched.

> Touch me.
> I have learnt the words
> *Habibi* and *Allah*
> and now you are both.
> I worship you to the point
> of wanting to devour
> your memories. I want to see

the little girl in your sleep
who carries a blanket
and walks this city.
I want this schizophrenic
city of yours. I don't sleep.
You say the only thing you know
is how to destroy men.
I am not scared. You scare me.
I want the smell
of the alleys
that inhabit you.
Is it blood you want? Is it my fingers
on your walls, between your legs?
You say telling is only
sweeter, and untrue. Touch me
then. With your memories,
your fingernails, with whatever lives inside
those dark tunnel-eyes of yours.

The ceiling is leaking. Drop the goddamn
camera. You are always shocked at how
things don't work here. I left my husband long before
I told him I would, kept asking him to sleep with me
every night. Every night. It was like digging,
to make love and love and love as if
the sun is buried underneath it all, and then
to look up and find yourself standing

in your own grave. The ceiling is leaking.
I left my husband—he was too Arab for me.
For God's sake get a bucket, a towel.
Drop the goddamn camera.
You are not Arab enough for me.

> You are beautiful and I am confused.
> I like it. I can't stop staring at you.
> I've read about you in books,
> in newspapers, in bodies on the TV screens.
> I've memorized all your names.
> I thought it would be easy
> to exile myself in your hips, your hair.
> I want to take photographs of you
> sleeping and covered
> naked and awake.
> I can't believe I have touched you.

You haven't.

> But, you liked it.

Yes. Do it again.

> Let me place my palm on your throat.
> Talk. I want to feel the tremors
> of your voice. Scream.
> Your hands, I love
> that they are bigger than mine.
> I want to unzip your dress, your spine.

You will find nothing in there. All those
war memories you hunger for,
they are not mine. I was too young,
remember only what I was told. You are chasing
the phantom of a phantom.
One night under the ground
the mothers kept singing.
They would have done it in a café in Paris.
They would have done it in a shelter in Baghdad.
I could have kissed you a thousand years ago.
It is the same scene everywhere and always,
give or take the sound of bullets.

You are my anvil. I cannot move.
Smile again. I love your
angel angel angel angel angel
teeth.

I dream of the whale every night.
I have seen it when we sailed the Mediterranean.
One refugee told me he only sees the dead now
when he looks at the sea. I dream of the whale.
I have seen it dip and emerge—
silent island, wing-tail, wing-fins.
And a mouth that swallows everything.

I love how you keep smoking.
Do all Arab women smoke like that?
I love that you call me *habibi*.

Arab women call everyone *habibi*.
Will you ever look at my body, not see
a map of your own longing?
I could get used to those light eyes of yours,
habibi, but your skin is too pale.
What a pretty little boy. Where were you born?
Paris? London? New York? It doesn't matter.
I've never been to any of them.
I will other you anyway, conquer you, and tomorrow
I will say, "Somewhere West. Too cute, too pale.
I don't remember his name."

> Tell me
> your name.
> Show me
> your legs.
> Open
> your mouth.
> What is it that Fairuz is singing?

Ahwak bila amali—
I love you without hope.

> Dance for me.

Stop asking me to dance
to Fairuz. I have done it last night,

I have been doing it forever. My wrists,
my arms are tired of her voice.
I prefer Umm Kulthum—
no one has ever screamed
about freedom the way she did,
except, perhaps, for Piaf (who has hands
the size of continents, eyebrows
like distant bird wings), and Dalida
(who has killed herself).

    Hold me.
    Why is there always the sound of cars
    on this street below us, in this empty city?
    What are these holes along your shoulder blades?

These are for my wings.

    Did they fall out?

No, they are beginning to sprout.

I was in love with a god of an Arab man once.
First he was my father, but he kept
cheating on me with other women.
My mother threatened and forgave, threatened and forgave.
He broke all the chairs and knelt before her.
The coffee is boiling. All this eternity is tiring.

I was in love with a god of an Arab man once.
He was too beautiful to love me back. I would have let him
flatten me, I would have let him wear me.
But he got on a plane and learnt
some European language and sent photos
of his half-European children.
Turn down the fire and lift the kettle.
All this eternity is tiring.
My feet are killing me.

    Let me touch
    your feet. I love your soles.
    Let me press my thumb
    into your calves.

Perhaps, one day, all I ever wanted
was to live with you. See here, look,
I grow heavy. I have a few white hairs.
Perhaps I'll dye them orange.
I am scared my children would forget
about me. Were I not afraid
of metros and airports, I would have left.

    Show me
    the scar under
    your belly button, above—

The only Western god I've ever loved
is Elvis. He does everything
passionately well. First he was too
beautiful. Then he was too ugly.
No one is ever sure whether or not
he is mortal. No, I don't have sugar
in the cupboards. There are no cupboards.
There is no tea here, only coffee.

There is a city under the ground
in some desert. There are bodies.
I will love you there.

      I will love you anywhere. I will take you
      anywhere. I will give you everything.

Men have always given me everything.
One of my lovers brought a box once.
He said, "Look, what a cute little puppy."
It wasn't. It was a ferocious, pitiful thing.

      Sing again. I want to live inside
      your voice, your strange accent, your shadow.

Turn off the lights. They keep blinking.
It feels like a goddamn interrogation room.
Get the candles, but not because I love you.
Get the candles, but not because I love you.

See how pretty you are tonight.

Drop the goddamn camera.

See how pretty you are tonight.

My eyes are not city lights.
I am not stronger than this dark.

See how pretty you are tonight.

The wine is in the fridge, *habibi*,
the ants are on the floor.
Pour me a glass and stay.
Pour me a glass and leave.

4
ADHAN
أذان

MAQAM

If I die, you say you will let your hair
turn silver, grow long, and you will go
into the dark place, for you've already begun
to forget what Mecca means.

Where we come from, you and I,
maqam means home, means music; the Qur'an
can only be read as a song; a sheikh recites the *Fatiha*
as if he has built a house among the lines, the *ayas*.

We've both called our daughters Aya, and when they ask
about their name, we play holy verses for them, listen
to how the sheikh lingers long enough on each letter,
how the audience claps and whistles—*Is it Umm Kulthum?*

our daughters ask. He knows all his *maqamat*,
this sheikh, says *God is greater,* and *Allah, Allah,*
reply the faithful and the unfaithful alike,
for the earth is such a small planet, and look,

there is Ithaca, almost always on the horizon—
float, my friend. Ithaca—*It is rough, but raises good*
men, says Homer, but oh, the women, the women
know how to house the bodies of the drowned. They sing,

In the Name of the Cross, of God the Merciful. A child
in Syria has amputated legs because he has ventured

into a minefield to eat grass. He still has two eyes,
two arms, a mouth. *God is greater, is greater*, stay

with me in the light a little longer. You light two cigarettes
at the same time, give me one. Tomorrow you will fly to Lesbos
to translate. The refugees will say *shai*, and you will say
tea, home, Mecca, Ithaca, maqam, maqam, maqam.

QUDUD VARIATIONS

Dear Aleppo, no moon tonight
nor my lover's cheek
        above the palm trees.

There were six of us
now there are five
        by the river.

In the garden of our language, a beggar
is he who waits to reap a kiss
        at my door.

Did they have to bomb your body
open, to behold Allah
        in your artery?

I should tell him a kiss is *haram* on a Friday.
Instead, we count the deaths, bright
        above the palm trees.

In the currency of love, her teeth
are pearls. He collects them
        by the river.

If we played the *ney* would we
resurrect the bulbul buried
        at my door?

Dear Aleppo, what *qudud* now
to measure the breath, the percussion
        in your artery?

THIS COUNTRY: GHAZAL FOR ABDEL HALIM HAFEZ

Time has come knocking on my door, and I've told him there's no healing
      this country.
I've loved and I've forgotten. *Hozn* isn't merely sadness—she can cling,
      this country.

Onstage, I gather *hozn* with my hands, gesturing here, and here,
and here my mother died three days after I was born to sing this country.

I've written letters from underneath the water. I've grown gills. I've waited
a long time in my backstage womb before my first breath, my beginning,
      this country.

My first concert was on a rooftop, like moonlight, like flocks of
      home-bred pigeons.
Later I became a dark nightingale. No one could stop my heart from conquering
      this country.

When Abdel Nasser was defeated, I sang that *Masr* was washing her hair
      by the water,
the same water that has gifted me my disease. Still, she loves the morning,
      this country.

I traced a line from the Qur'an in the air the last time I left for a hospital
      in London. Girls threw
themselves off balconies the day I died. She has beautiful ways of keening,
      this country.

One of my songs ends with Laughter and starts with Love. Sing it.
    I had a radio
near my hospital bed. I could hear Cairo clearly, could hear her ring,
    this country.

GHAZAL: SAMIRA TAWFIQ SINGS A LOVE POEM

I count the stars and place them in my hand, my heart.
They're odd, they're even. They say nothing'll go as we planned, my heart.

Spare me this city made of *tibr*. "I will desert this castle,
go back to that house of poetry" and sand—my heart.

All day I pretend to collect water, for a glimpse of his dark
skin. The bridges almost break; they can't withstand my heart.

I was a little girl who sang in a tree. Now, before the afternoon and after
sunset and between the two, people listen for my chant, my heart.

My smile lies and tells the truth. The audience loves my glitter, my kohl,
my shoulder pads, the mole on my left cheek, my wink, and my heart.

The young artists sing my songs. That's fine. But they should ask first.
After all, I've never been afraid of love, never banned my heart.

My stage name, *Tawfiq*, means success. But I don't want to sing
anymore. I'm sad for Lebanon, Syria—the land, my heart.

UMM KULTHUM SPEAKS

I was a little boy with the voice of a god
once. How else could my father set this spell of mine
free? So I dressed my voice, first with boy's clothing,
then with the Qur'an, then with poems, then with Egypt,
but all these were merely pretexts
for the magic that rose out of my throat.
Don't you see how the streets are empty
on my radio Thursdays? Do you know what *tarab*
means? To repeat, to carry everyone back
to their hurt. I bent the sentences I sang
into portals, and what else could you have screamed
but *Allah Allah Allah* for hours?
Then came the scarf in my left hand,
the black diamond-studded cat-eye sunglasses,
but these were things I carried because
they had names. One has to dress
for this earth. You still haven't seen my wings.
I haven't been called a planet for nothing. My voice soars
around the theater, the sun, and comes back to this street
at midnight, more than half a century later, asking,
Has love ever seen such drunkenness?
Everything about me orbits. Even my coffin
has sailed the streets of Cairo for hours.

MESSAGES IN THE DARK

The text messages move   across the bottom of the TV screen   I watch

Umm Kulthum sing   *Far from You*   & Tarek sends   *I adore you Nariman*

followed by Count Mo's *the stars . . . the stars . . .*   Nadine's *U R My MoOn*

Najla's *I am burning*   Umm Kulthum sings *Longing*   Khaled writes *I love*

my wife very much   Majed wants to meet *a pretty girl*   Waleed wants God

to protect Syria & its people   Romantic Knight swears he is *very sorry*

Anonymous screams *Long Live Egypt*   Painter & Poet sends *For EvArrrr*

Umm Kulthum repeats her   آه آه   Hind the Wounded pines for *true love*

so does University Teacher   every now and then there's the word   CONTROL

which means no messages for a second   then Liqaa' asks *Where r u?*

Kareem goes *Get well soon Jiji*   Hipster shouts *What's up Umm K?*

the diva answers   *My life is torture*   *Salaam from Palestine* types Omar

& Fahd calls *everyone to prayer may God forgive us all*   Ahmad Imad

Foufou Kamal want *to connect with Divorced Lady*   *Happy birthday mama*

says Sadek   *You are the garlic of my heart*   Someone wishes everyone

A morning of roses and carnations   Insomniac *can't sleep*   Umm K. chants

Remember   Rami says *Baghdad is sad today* after which   CONTROL

Divorced Lady can we meet?   *I dedicate this song to all of you watching*

Adel types *ya batta* Ali asks Hanan if he can know her *real name* Umm K.

is melting *Mabrook mabrook for the bride & groom Egypt Egypt Egypt Egypt*

Painter & Poet is back he is *afraid of the happiness a phone call might bring*

Lover is drunk asks his mother to forgive him Umm Kulthum's voice soars

trembles the text messages keep rolling on their invisible wheels آه آه you

invisible wheels of hope transport us beyond these small living rooms of longing

FI YOM WI LEILA

Spare me this Arab love for dictators tonight.
Come closer, listen—Warda is singing,
Fi Yom Wi Leila. This day, this night, let us.
Push this talk of the land to the side. Spare me
this Arab love for conspiracy tonight. Lower your voice
to the sound of my pupils. Look at me. Let's music
instead, let's cigarette, let's wine and laughter. Let's call
friends. Remember how our mothers used to serve
cigarette packs on trays to their guests?
Fi Marlboro, fi Viceroy, fi Gitanes, they said.
Every house had them cigarette trays. Some nights the politics
settled with the ashes, and the jokes came, the clapping,
the *Allah Allah* rising with the smoke, the dancing. Time tortures
everyone. Let's heal a little. Ask me if I could ever
love again. Let's exaggerate. Ask me if there will ever be
arms like mine. Warda is singing she'd been missing you
long before she'd met you. I missed you before I met you too.
And now, *habibi,* even more, even more.

3ARABI SONG

"Good morning, God,"
Mom explained, "is what he's saying here."
Some year in the '80s, the whole town sang
"*Lasciatemi Cantare*," though no one understood
the lyrics. But my mother, who had learnt
a little Italian with the nuns at school,
pointed out, "Here, he's saying *Buongiorno Dio*,
good morning, God." Dad noted
the words *piano piano* and *Maria*,
said perhaps it was the mother of Jesus.

My father had a way of clapping
with one hand: he'd open and close it,
making his fingers touch his palm—the sound
a bit like smacking your lips. It was as if he was
half clapping, half calling you to come closer,
as he sang Edith Piaf's "Padam Padam,"
which became an Arabic "*param, param, param.*"

My aunt, his sister, loved Aznavour.
She made me promise I'd take her to a concert of his
when I grew up, and that he'd sing
that song about knowing how to smile
just for her. They all believed

they had a Dalida within them—
blonde, fine, mélancolique, méditerranéenne,

and of course "*malade, complètement malade,*"
with always "*ya baladi*" at the tip of her tongue.
And when they did remember *baladi*, our country,

was tearing itself apart,
when they remembered the childhood
lost, wanted it back,
they listened to Remi Bandali.
As the little girl sang about *salaam*,
I told my brother I wanted to be
an Arabic dancer, a *razassa*,
that I preferred *Sesame Street*'s song,
and went la-la-la-la-la-la-la-la-ing down the corridor.

By the end of the '90s, that remake of
the Guevara song had conquered
the Arab world. We teenagers danced to it,
guessed at the words
bravura, la muerte, revolucionario.
We also discovered Queen, wanted
"to break free, God knows," God knows

every song, every hurt
we were about to witness
would have a *tam tam ta ta tam*
derbakkeh beat in quarter notes,
would speak
of the price of bread,

the broken furniture on the street,
the tap water we cannot drink, and
(*tam tam ta ta tam*, let's give it
a shoulder shake too)
this *revolución*
we keep longing for with a

Buongiorno Dio
we are the children
with *param param* hearts
full of stories do you remember
ya baladi open Sesame
hasta siempre we want
to break free
dear Che Maria *piano piano*

PIANO

Dear God,
I heard the children of Yarmouk
have eaten the tree birds. By this I mean
how are you?

Dear God,
Do you have a piano? By this I mean
the kind that licks your heart clean
the way the sun burns & brightens
the sky, even after night raids.

Dear God,
Do you wait? By this I mean
hell here has a vestibule—in it
Aeham plays the piano. He calls it
The Piano of the Siege, calls it
Brother. By this he means
even the dried pit of a song
is country, is food for now.

Dear God,
Do you have streets? Here in the camps,
we name our streets after the cities
we've lost. By this I mean we have heard
the rivers of our cities call us
like blind old women in empty living rooms.

Dear God,
I love you. By this I mean
do you have another name?
By this I mean there are armies
who shout your name & burn houses
& pianos. Come back.

Dear God,
Yesterday I saw a fish flailing
in the mouth of a seagull.
For a moment it seemed the bird
was choking, the fish diving upward
for air. By this I mean
do you see us dance?

CARIOCA

For Taheyya Carioca, Egyptian dancer

If you want to walk THE ROAD
of LOVE & MADNESS, start
with good knees. I was twelve when I ran
barefoot to a train station
villages away—ADIEU BONAPARTE.
If you want to know how smart a woman is,
consider her eyes. Ask her if she would slap
a tyrant. Ask her if she would cry when
THE WATER CARRIER IS DEAD.

I took that train and left
for ISKANDARIYYA, AGAIN & FOREVER.
Only MY FATHER DECEIVED ME, but now
I can tell a man's character by his teeth,
his fingernails. I CAN'T remember the order
of my husbands, but oh how I LOVE
DANCE. I LOVE MISTAKES (sin, even)
but will not forgive ungraceful hands.
Do you want to see what my hands can do
with a sword? Play some music. LONG LIVE ART.

The first time I performed in Casino Badia,
Huriyya went into the dressing room and tore
my outfit to pieces. But PATIENCE
IS BEAUTIFUL (delicious, even).
I learnt the carioca and it gave me

its name. I became THE PRINCESS
OF THE ISLAND, my island,
for marriage ends, and A WOMAN'S YOUTH
ends, and I was never in it for THE MARKET
OF WOMEN, and I was never on the lookout
for IBN EL HALAL either. IS IT MY FAULT
the body wants to undulate, to pray?
If you ask what my favorite dance is,
go to the temple. Listen.
Now slowly lift your arms.

BODY

For Hasan Rabeh, young dancer displaced from Syria, who killed himself by jumping from a 7th-floor balcony in Beirut, Wednesday, June 22, 2016

& perhaps you flew. I read the news, how you plunged from the 7th floor,
       a Beirut balcony,
& I am filled with a sound of sirens, a need to be alone. This war this theater
       this city this.
& I was at a da Vinci exhibit at the museum this morning.
& what a blessing, to say I was at a da Vinci exhibit this morning.
& he was a pacifist who designed killing machines, for money always comes
       from warlords.
& he, who like no other knew of the divine proportions of the body,
& he who preferred to trace limbs & ligaments
& the glide of bat wings in the air, he who preferred the theater,
& the projector, & the drum, & bridges, imagined the machine gun,
& the submarine, & the tank, sculpted a bullet with a more precise dance.
& oh how the mind bends & how light & shadows fall.
& you, young dancer, tell me, what do you know of the flight of birds,
& of the difference between theatricality & war, dissection & witchcraft,
       dance & death?
& were you searching for your Palestine in Damascus, for your Damascus
       in Beirut,
& were you looking for Allah in the joint, the spine, the twirl?
& that last scribble your body made in the air, was that you,
& were you trying to write backward, to lift instead?
& did you? Tell me, are the mountains blue in the distance?
& does poetry matter, & does dance?
& is there a bridge where the displaced go after they're gone?

ADHAN

There is something about the *adhan* at dawn, how it lifts
your head from your pillow; how it pulls
you from sleep like a bucket from a dark
well, heavy with the same wish to fall;
how when the sky is still full of shadows, it calls
that prayer is better than sleep
(and there's something Shakespearean
about it, and something modern);
how the voices rise now
from different speakers in different mosques—
Allahu Akbar, Allahu Akbar, an unsynchronized
Greek chorus that glazes the city, reaches
the gutters, the babies in their cots, the thieves, repeats
Prayer is better than sleep, as if
*The world is beautiful and full of sunrises, prayer
is better than sleep,* so you grip
your lover's arm, the book on your bedside table,
your cigarette pack, your blanket, as if
Yes, I heard you. Hallelujah. Amen. Amen.

NOTES

p. 11—"Broken Ghazal: Speak Arabic"
Sheikh Imam was an Egyptian singer and composer (1918–1995), famous for his po-
litically engaged, satirical songs, and his collaboration with Egyptian colloquial poet
Ahmed Fouad Negm.

p. 13—*Shafaq* is Arabic for "twilight."

p. 18—"You Fixed It"
Hafiz refers to Hafiz al-Assad, Syrian president at the time. | *Ya hala* means "welcome"
in Arabic. | *Crépuscule* and شفق are French and Arabic for "twilight." | *Lahm bi ʿajeen* is
a kind of Arabic meat pie.

pp. 20-21—"My Town"
Ummi is Arabic for "mother." | *Barazeq* is a kind of Arabic sweet. | *ʿaross* is Arabic for
"bride." | *Kaak* is a kind of bread sprinkled with sesame seeds, usually sold by street
vendors. | *Chocolat mou* is a dessert made of chocolate ice cream, whipped cream, and
chocolate sauce. The reference here is also to a famous *chocolat mou* place in Tripoli, Leb-
anon, called "*Chocolat Mou* Kingdom." | The burnt books are a reference to the burning
of Tripoli's Saeh Library, in January 2014.

pp. 25-29—"3amto"
3amto is Arabic for "aunt," specifically the father's sister. It is written in Arabizi. In this
poem, the words *wara2 3enab, yil3an abooki,* and *ya 3uyuni inti* are also written in Arabizi.
| *Habibti* is Arabic for "my love," when the speaker is addressing a female. Its masculine
form is *habibi*, although it is common to use *habibi* for both men and women. | *Fattoush*
is a Lebanese salad. | *Hamdillah* is Arabic for "thank God." | *Wara2 3enab* is a dish of
stuffed vine leaves. | *Yil3an abooki* is an Arabic curse that would literally translate as
"goddamn your father," used here in an endearing way. | *Ya 3uyuni inti* is Arabic "you
are my eyes." | *Akh* is a sigh sound. | *Kibbeh* is a Lebanese dish that consists of minced

meat, bulgur, onion, and some seasoning. | *Ayat al-Kursi* is verse 255 of the second *surah* (chapter) of the Qur'an. Literally translated as "The Verse of the Throne." | Laban is Arabic for "yogurt."

p. 30—"Dismantling Grief"
Darwish is in reference to Palestinian poet Mahmoud Darwish, and Julia refers to Julia Boutros, Lebanese singer.

p. 31—*Ya'aburnee* (Arabic): literally "you bury me," a term of endearment expressing the desire to die before a loved one, rather than live without him or her.

pp. 40-42—"And Still, the Sun"
Each one-line stanza in this poem is the first line of the successive stanzas of Pablo Neruda's "Walking Around." | *Zaatar* is a mixture of dried, crushed thyme, sesame seeds, sumac, and salt. It's often mixed with olive oil and eaten with bread. | Teita is Arabic for "grandmother."

p. 48—"Ghazal: This *Hijra*"
Hijra literally translates as "migration," and is used here to mean displacement. In an Islamic context, *Hijra* is a reference to the journey that the prophet Muhammad made from Mecca to Medina, because he was being persecuted. | The poem is dedicated to thousands of Yazidis and Christians who fled their Iraqi hometowns of Sinjar and Mosul in the summer of 2014, in fear of being killed by ISIS. | The expression "*Ya* Sayyab" is a reference to Badr Shakir al-Sayyab, Iraqi poet, and his famous poem "Rain Song."

p. 49—"Ghazal: Back Home"
Bahr is Arabic for "sea." Also, in Arabic poetry, *bahr* means "meter."

pp. 50-56—"Naming Things"
Some images in this poem refer to newspaper and TV reports on the refugee crisis. | رحلنا is Arabic for "We have left." | Aeham refers to Aeham Ahmad, the Palestinian pianist who played the piano in the besieged Yarmouk camp. ISIS burnt his piano and he

left for Germany. | و ما أطال النوم عمراً is a line from *The Rubaiyat of Omar al-Khayyam,* famously sung by Umm Kulthum. | The words *ra7eel, 3awda,* and *3arabi* are written in Arabizi, and they are Arabic for "departure," "returning," and "Arabic."

p. 57—*Ahwak* is Arabic for "I love you."

p. 58—"Louder than Hearts and *Derbakkehs*"
A *derbakkeh* is a small drum used in Arabic music. | *Yalla* is Arabic for "Come on."

pp. 60-61—"The Woman in Our House" and "Wallada bint al-Mustakfi Speaks"
Wallada bint al-Mustakfi was an Andalusian poet who lived in eleventh-century Córdoba. The daughter of an Umayyad caliph, she inherited his palace and created a literary salon there. She was the lover of Ibn Zaydún, famous Arab poet. She was known for being bold, beautiful, and intelligent. Her name, Wallada, is Arabic for "bearer of children."

p. 63—"*Majnun*"
Majnun is Arabic for "crazy," and refers here to the seventh-century Arabic poet, Qays bin al-Mulawwah. He is known as "*Majnun* Layla," which is Arabic for "crazy about Layla." The story is that Qays bin al-Mulawwah fell in love with Layla, but her father didn't allow them to get married. He is said to have lost his mind and exiled himself into the wilderness, where he spent his time composing love poems for her. This poem references some anecdotes about the two lovers. | The name Layla means "one night."

p. 65—"Ode to my Non-Arabic Lover"
Dabkeh is a Lebanese folk dance. | Fairuz is a famous Lebanese diva. For Umm Kulthum, see notes below to "Umm Kulthum Speaks." | *Ooff ooff ooff* are words sung at the beginning of a *mawwal,* the sound of them implying pain or suffering. A *mawwal* is an Arabic genre of vocal music that is performed before the actual song begins.

p. 66—"My Non-Arabic Lover and I Take the Train"
Orloj refers to the medieval astronomical clock in Prague.

p. 67—"نوم"

نوم is Arabic for "sleep."

pp. 68–76—*"Khandaq Mon Amour"*

Khandaq is Arabic for "trench." The title takes after Marguerite Duras's *Hiroshima Mon Amour*.

p. 78—*"Maqam"*

Maqam (plural *maqamat*) is the system of melodic modes used in traditional Arabic music. The word *maqam* in Arabic also means place. | The *Fatiha (al-Fatiha)* is the first *surah* (chapter) of the Qur'an.

p. 80—*"Qudud* Variations"

The word *Qudud* refers here to *Qudud Halabiyya*, which would literally translate as "musical measures from Aleppo." The *Qudud* is a form of traditional music and singing from Syria. The poem plays on the images traditionally found in the *Qudud* and inverts them. | The *ney* is a kind of flute in Middle Eastern music.

p. 82—"This Country: Ghazal for Abdel Halim Hafez"

Abdel Halim Hafez was one of the most popular Egyptian singers, very well-known across the Arab world. He died in 1977 at age 47 in London, where he was undergoing treatment for bilharzia, which he had caught as a child. He was nicknamed "the Dark Nightingale." Stanzas 1, 3, 5, and 7 contain references to his songs. | The word *hozn* is Arabic for "sadness," and *Masr* is Arabic for "Egypt."

p. 84—"Ghazal: Samira Tawfiq Sings a Love Poem"

Samira Tawfiq (born 1935) is a well-known Lebanese singer. Stanzas 1, 2, 3, and 4 contain references to some of her songs. | *Tibr* is Arabic for "gold."

p. 85—"Umm Kulthum Speaks"

Umm Kulthum was an Egyptian singer, one of the most famous divas in the Arab world. When she was young, her father used to take her singing dressed as a boy. | *Tarab* is a kind of Arabic music. The word is also used to describe the emotional effect of this kind of music on the listener, who is almost in a state of trance. | Umm Kulthum was given the title of *Kawkab Al Sharq*, which literally means "Planet of the East," more often translated as "Star of the East." | *"Has love ever seen such drunkenness?"* is a reference to a line from an Umm Kulthum song.

p. 86—"Messages in the Dark"
Batta is Arabic for "duck," and is often used to describe a cute girl. | *Mabrook* is Arabic for "congratulations." | آ reads as "ah," and is sung as a sigh.

p. 88—*"Fi Yom Wi Leila"*
Warda refers to Warda Al Jazairia, famous Algerian singer. *Fi Yom Wi Leila* is also the title of one of her songs, and it translates as "in a day and a night." | *Fi Marlboro, fi Viceroy, fi Gitanes* means "there's Marlboro, there's Viceroy, there's Gitanes."

pp. 89-91—"*3arabi* Song"
3arabi is the Arabizi way of writing "Arabic." | *Baladi* is Arabic for "my country." | Remi Bandali was a Lebanese child singer in the '80s, famous for her trilingual song, loosely translated as "Give Us Back Our Childhood."

p. 92—"Piano"
This poem refers again to the pianist of Yarmouk, Aeham Ahmad.

p. 94—"Carioca"
Taheyya Carioca was a famous Egyptian belly dancer and actress. The words in caps are titles of movies in which she acted. | *Ibn el Halal* literally means "the *halal* son," one conceived in marriage, but also refers here to a good man.

ACKNOWLEDGMENTS

Shukran to the editors of the journals and anthologies in which the following poems first appeared (sometimes in earlier versions):

32 Poems: "Adhan"; *Boulevard*: "Majnun," "*Fi Yom Wi Leila*"; *Calyx*: "*3amto*," "Umm Kulthum Speaks"; *The Common*: "My Town," "Pizza with Lightbulb"; *Copper Nickel*: "And Still, the Sun"; *Dove Tales*: "Inside Out"; *Ecotone:* "Listen," "The Woman in Our House," "Asmahan"; *Electronic Intifada*: "Inside Out"; *HeArt*: "Thirty-two and in a Different Country"; *The Margins:* "I Dreamt We Threw Bread Crumbs," "Louder than Hearts and *Derbakkehs*"; *The Midwest Quarterly*: "Ghazal: The Dead"; *The Missing Slate*: "*Fi Yom Wi Leila*"; *Mslexia*: "After the Explosions"; *One*: "Dismantling Grief"; *One Throne*: "Terror/Mathematics"; *The Orison Anthology*: "Adhan"; *Paris Lit Up:* "Ghazal: Samira Tawfiq Sings a Love Poem," "*3arabi* Song"; *Poetry*: "Maqam," *Rattle*: "Ya'aburnee," "Ghazal: Back Home," "This Country: Ghazal for Abdel Halim Hafez"; *Resisting Arrest: Songs to Stretch the Sky:* "Dismantling Grief"; *The Rialto*: "Naming Things," "Ode to My Non-Arabic Lover," "My Non-Arabic Lover and I Take the Train," "*Khandaq Mon Amour*"; *River Styx:* "You Fixed It"; *Rusted Radishes*: "Relentless"; *The Well Review:* "نوم"; *Washington Square Review:* "Broken Ghazal: Speak Arabic," "Piano"; *Watching the Perseids: The Backwaters Press Twentieth Anniversary Anthology:* "Ghazal: This *Hijra,*" "My Non-Arabic Lover and I Take the Train"; *World Literature Today*: "Body."

Many of these poems appeared in the chapbook *3arabi Song*, winner of the 2016 Rattle Chapbook Prize. I am thankful to Timothy Green for believing in them.

I send gratitude and love to: my family and friends—I couldn't have worked on these poems had it not been for your love and support; my friend Frank Dullaghan, who listened to most of these poems in their early stages; the team at Bauhan Publishing; Betsy Sholl for believing in this book; the people who have listened to many of these poems at poetry readings before they were published; my hometown Tripoli, Lebanon; and you, reader—thank you.

The May Sarton New Hampshire Poetry Prize

The May Sarton New Hampshire Poetry Prize is named for May Sarton, the renowned novelist, memoirist, poet, and feminist (1912–1995) who lived for many years in Nelson, New Hampshire, not far from Peterborough, home of William L. Bauhan Publishing. In 1967, she approached Bauhan and asked him to publish her book of poetry, *As Does New Hampshire*. She wrote the collection to celebrate the bicentennial of Nelson, and dedicated it to the residents of the town.

May Sarton was a prolific writer of poetry, novels, and perhaps what she is best known for— nonfiction on growing older (*Recovering: A Journal, Journal of Solitude,* among others). She considered herself a poet first, though, and in honor of that and to celebrate the centenary of her birth in 2012, Sarah Bauhan, who inherited her father's small publishing company, launched the prize. (www.bauhanpublishing.com/may-sarton-prize)

PAST MAY SARTON WINNERS:

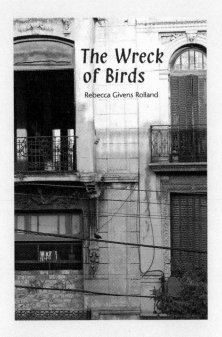

In *The Wreck of Birds*, the first winner of Bauhan Publishing's May Sarton New Hampshire Poetry Prize, Rebecca Givens Rolland embraces an assimilation of internal feeling and thought with circumstances of the natural world and the conflicts and triumphs of our human endeavors. Here, we discover a language that seeks to at once replicate and transcend experiences of loss and disaster, and together with the poet "we hope that such bold fates will not forget us." Even at the speaker's most vulnerable moments, when "Each word we'd spoken / scowls back, mirrored in barrels of wind" these personal poems insist on renewal. With daring honesty and formal skill, *The Wreck of Birds* achieves a revelatory otherness—what Keats called the "soul-making task" of poetry.

—Walter E. Butts, New Hampshire Poet Laureate (2009–2013), and author of *Cathedral of Nervous Horses: New and Selected Poems,* and *Sunday Evening at the Stardust Café*

Rebecca Givens Rolland is a speech-language pathologist and doctoral student at the Harvard Graduate School of Education. Her poetry has previously appeared in journals including *Colorado Review, American Letters & Commentary, Denver Quarterly, Witness, and the Cincinnati Review,* and she is the recipient of the Andrew W. Mellon Fellowship, the Clapp Fellowship from Yale University, an Academy of American Poets Prize, and the Dana Award.

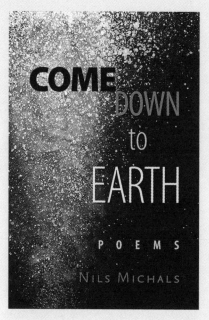

Nils Michals won the second May Sarton New Hampshire Poetry Prize in 2012, and has also written the book *Lure*, which won the Lena-Miles Wever Todd award in 2004. His poetry has been featured in *The Bacon Review, diode, White Whale Review, Bay Poetics, The Laurel Review* and *Sonora Review*. He lives in Santa Cruz, California and teaches at West Valley College.

Nils Michals is alternately healed and wounded by the tension between the timeless machinations of humankind and the modern machinery that lifts us beyond—and plunges us back to—our all-too-human, earthly selves. Supported by minimally narrative, page-oriented forms, his poems transcribe poetry's intangibles—love, loss, hope, a sense of the holy—in a language located somewhere between devotional and raw, but they mourn and celebrate as much of what is surreal in today's news as of what is familiar in the universal mysteries . . . *Come Down to Earth* is a 'long villa with every door thrown open' "

—Alice B. Fogel, New Hampshire Poet Laureate (2014-2019), and author of *Strange Terrain: A Poetry Handbook for The Reluctant Reader* and *Be That Empty*

David Koehn won the third May Sarton New Hampshire Poetry Prize in 2013. His poetry and translations were previously collected in two chapbooks, *Tunic,* (speCt! books 2013) a small collection of some of his translations of *Catullus,* and *Coil* (University of Alaska, 1998), winner of the Midnight Sun Chapbook Contest. He lives with his family in Pleasanton, California.

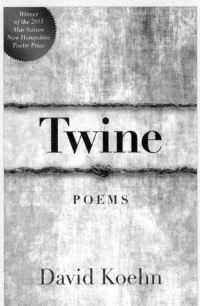

David Koehn's first book, *Twine,* never falters—one strong poem after another. This is the work of a mature poet. His use of detail is not only precise and evocative; it's transformative."
—JEFF FRIEDMAN, 2013 May Sarton New Hampshire Poetry Prize judge and author of *Pretenders*

David Koehn's imagination, rambunctious and abundant, keeps its footing: a sense of balance like his description of fishing: "Feeling the weight . . . of the measurement of air." That sense of weight and air, rhythm and fact, the ethereal and the brutal, animates images like boxers of the bare-fist era: "Hippo-bellied/And bitter, bulbous in their bestiary masks." An original and distinctively musical poet.

—ROBERT PINSKY,
United States Poet Laureate, 1997-2000
and author of *Selected Poems,* among numerous other collections

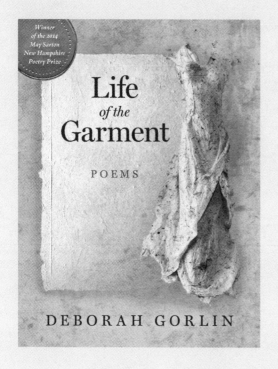

Winner
of the 2014
May Sarton
New Hampshire
Poetry Prize

Life
of the
Garment

POEMS

DEBORAH GORLIN

Deborah Gorlin won the 2014 May Sarton New Hampshire Poetry Prize. She has published in *Poetry, Antioch Review, American Poetry Review, Seneca Review, The Massachusetts Review, The Harvard Review, Green Mountains Review, Bomb, Connecticut Review, Women's Review of Books, New England Review*, and *Best Spiritual Writing 2000*. Gorlin also won the 1996 White Pine Poetry Press Prize for her first book of poems, *Bodily Course*. She holds an MFA from the University of California/Irvine. Since 1991, she has taught writing at Hampshire College, where she serves as co-director of the Writing Program. She is currently a poetry editor at *The Massachusetts Review*.

In poem after poem in *Life of the Garment*, Deborah Gorlin clothes us in her fabric of sung words, with characters unique and familiar, and facsimiles of love that open and close their eyes, comfort, and gaze upon us. Read this fine collection—you will see for yourself.

—Gary Margolis, 2014 May Sarton New Hampshire Poetry Prize judge
and author of *Raking the Winter Leaves*.

Desirée Alvarez won the 2015 May Sarton New Hampshire Poetry Prize. She is a poet and painter who has received numerous awards for her written and visual work, including the Glenna Luschei Award from *Prairie Schooner*, the Robert D. Richardson Non-Fiction Award from *Denver Quarterly*, and the Willard L. Metcalf Award from the American Academy of Arts and Letters. She has published in *Poetry*, *Boston Review*, and *The Iowa Review*, and received fellowships from Yaddo, Poets House, and New York Foundation for the Arts. Alvarez received her MFA from School of Visual Arts and BA from Wesleyan University. Testing the boundaries of image and language through interdisciplinary work, as a visual poet she exhibits widely and teaches at CUNY, The Juilliard School, and Artists Space.

These poems often shot shivers up my spine. Some made me cry. This is a book I'll want to read over and over.

—Mekeel McBride, 2015 May Sarton New Hampshire Poetry Prize judge and author of *Dog Star Delicatessen: New and Selected Poems*

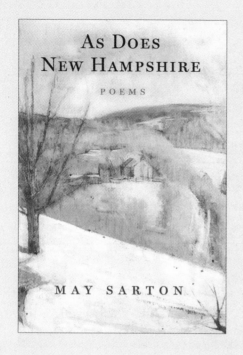

Bauhan Publishing is pleased to reissue May Sarton's *As Does New Hampshire* in 2017 to help celebrate the 250th anniversary of Nelson, New Hampshire, the village where Sarton lived for many years.

Born in Belgium, Sarton and her parents fled Europe in 1916 to settle in Cambridge, Massachusetts. After a particularly bleak period in her life, she moved to Nelson in the 1950s and found the small-town setting restorative in many ways. She originally published *As Does New Hampshire* in 1967 to honor of the village's bicentennial and dedicated it to "my neighbors."

A Glass of Water

Here is a glass of water from my well.
It tastes of rock and root and earth and rain;
It is the best I have, my only spell,
And it is cold, and better than champagne.
Perhaps someone will pass this house one day
To drink, and be restored, and go his way,
Someone in dark confusion as I was
When I drank down cold water in a glass,
Drank a transparent health to keep me sane,
After the bitter mood had gone again.

With titles such as "Reflections by a Fire," "Mud Season," "Still Life in a Snowstorm," "Apple Tree in May," "The Horse-Pulling," "A Late Mowing," and "Stone Walls" the poems in *As Does New Hampshire* evoke Sarton's experience living in rural New Hampshire. The collection was the inspiration for Bauhan Publishing's May Sarton New Hampshire Poetry Prize.